AROUND THE WORLD
and Back Again

A Travel Journal for Everyone
Who Loves to Get Away

KATE PETERSON

a TarcherPerigee book

tarcherperigee

an imprint of Penguin Random House LLC
penguinrandomhouse.com

TarcherPerigee with tp colophon is a registered trademark of Penguin Random House LLC

Most TarcherPerigee books are available at special quantity discounts for bulk purchase for sales promotions, premiums, fund-raising, and educational needs. Special books or book excerpts also can be created to fit specific needs. For details, write: SpecialMarkets @penguinrandomhouse.com.

ISBN 9780593418161

Printed in the United States of America
1st Printing

Book composition by Lorie Pagnozzi

FOR MY DAD,

who opened my eyes to travel
and never failed to bring
me back a Toblerone

INTRODUCTION

Hi! I'm Kate, and I'm a travel addict. I've traveled across Morocco by train in the middle of the night, sipped mind-blowing coffee in Colombia, and gone for a sunrise swim in the South China Sea. I've also mixed up the Greek verbs for "to have" and "to be," asked a waiter "Are you a restroom?," had a claustrophobic panic attack at the top of the Duomo in Florence and fallen down both immediately and spectacularly the second I got outside, and been electrocuted at a hotel in Thailand. (Trust me—always read the reviews!)

But those peaks and valleys are exactly what travel does best: it shakes you out of the steady medium of your everyday routine and creates room for highs and lows, for intense new flavors and surprising sights, for experiences that are unpredictable and vivid and extraordinary. It connects you to people and places outside your "normal," and expands your definition of it forever. And that's exactly why it's so good for us, and so good for the world.

In early March 2020, my husband and I were an hour from boarding a flight to Portugal when the Covid-19 European travel ban was issued. We blearily pulled our bags from the flight, never imagining that those headlines from abroad were about to take over the whole world for an entire year. When you have a year to think about travel without getting to do it, you have more time to think beyond what and where and more about why and how—and having spent 2020 staying home and making this book, I now have a greater sense of gratitude, respect, and awe for travel than ever before. Where I might have once complained about a long flight, I now feel amazed that we have the technology to fly long distances at all; and where I was once determined to explore as many new places as possible, I now find myself more drawn to the idea of really getting to know the places I've already been. I want to travel well, and with curiosity, and more thoughtfully than ever before. And I want to help you do that too.

In this book, I've aimed to strike a balance between fun checklists and thought-provoking journal prompts, and between lighthearted activity pages and others that dig deeper. I sincerely hope that you find it both entertaining and enlightening, and that you positively destroy it, filling its pages and spilling Cantonese wonton soup and Argentinian chimichurri sauce all over it as this journal travels with you around the world. Be a great time! Whoops—have a great time. And watch out for power lines after a monsoon.

Sincerely,
Kate
The travel addict who wrote this book

ALOHA, ARIGATO & ARRIVEDERCI

Use this page to list the words for "hello," "thank you," and "goodbye" in as many languages as possible for easy reference on the road.

LANGUAGE	HELLO	THANK YOU	GOODBYE

What do you think the difference is between a tourist and a traveler?

I ♥ SHIRTS THAT SAY WHAT I ♥

FAVORITE MAJOR SIGHTS I'VE SEEN

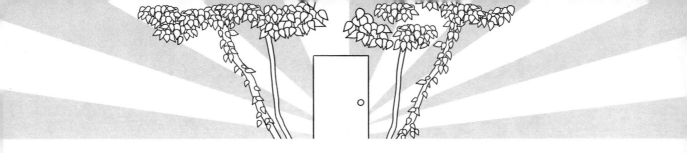

THE BEST HIDDEN GEMS I'VE FOUND

AROUND THE WORLD IN NINE BREAKFASTS

What's on your plate this morning? Draw your breakfast, then label each with the date and place where you ate it.

WORLD COFFEE & TEA CHECKLIST

date and location:

- ☐ *Café de olla*
- ☐ Italian espresso
- ☐ *Café bombón*
- ☐ Arabic coffee
- ☐ Café au lait
- ☐ Vietnamese egg coffee
- ☐ Café Touba
- ☐ Thai iced tea
- ☐ Matcha
- ☐ Moroccan mint tea
- ☐ Masala chai
- ☐ Yerba maté
- ☐ Southern sweet tea
- ☐ Earl Grey tea
- ☐ Bubble tea
- ☐
- ☐
- ☐

Reflect on an experience you had with a local while traveling. What did you learn from them? What would you say to them now if you could see them again?

_____
_____
_____
_____
_____
_____
_____
_____
_____
_____
_____
_____
_____
_____
_____
_____
_____
_____
_____
_____
_____
_____
_____

AIRPORT BINGO

SOMEONE USING THEIR BAG AS A PILLOW	A FURRY FRIEND IN A CARRYING CASE	A SNAZZY MATCHING SWEATSUIT	FAKE PLANTS	SOMEONE CHUGGING THEIR WATER BEFORE SECURITY
MONO-GRAMMED LUGGAGE	AN OUT-OF-ORDER RESTROOM OR WATER FOUNTAIN	SPEEDING AIRPORT CART	HEARING THE SAME RECORDED MESSAGE 5+ TIMES	A LINE WITH 20 OR MORE PEOPLE IN IT
A TOURIST WEARING A T-SHIRT FROM THE PLACE YOU'RE IN	MOVING-WALKWAY TRAFFIC JAM		NECK PILLOW AS FASHION ACCESSORY	SOMEONE RUNNING TO CATCH THEIR FLIGHT
LICENSE PLATE NAME SOUVENIRS	FREEZING A/C OR SWELTERING HEATING	BAFFLING SIGNAGE	SOMEONE SPEAKING A LANGUAGE YOU DON'T UNDERSTAND	A CURRENCY EXCHANGE KIOSK
MICROWAVED FOOD	SOMEONE DRESSED FOR A TROPICAL VACATION	SOMEONE GETTING THEIR SHOES SHINED	A GROUP IN MATCHING T-SHIRTS	SPORTS EQUIPMENT OR MUSICAL INSTRUMENT

WHAT'S IN YOUR CARRY-ON?

DRAW AND LABEL ALL
YOUR TRAVEL ESSENTIALS

GLOBETROTTER CHALLENGE
LEVEL 1

- ■ Pack only a carry-on for an international trip

- ■ Greet your server, order your meal, and get the check in a foreign language

- ■ Mail a letter to a friend from a post office in another country

- ■ Master the use of chopsticks and the proper etiquette for eating with them

- ■ Get around on public transit for an entire day while traveling

- ■ Bring home a souvenir made from start to finish in the place you're visiting

Write about a trip that turned out totally different from your expectations. Did you learn anything from the experience?

_____
_____
_____
_____
_____
_____
_____
_____
_____
_____
_____
_____
_____
_____
_____
_____
_____
_____
_____
_____
_____
_____
_____

DETOUR

I'M ON A BOAT

Destination:

Origin:

What kind of boat are you on?

Who are you traveling with?

How early did you get up this morning?

Three words to describe how you're feeling:

How are you passing the time on the boat?

How seasick are you right now, on a scale from 1–5?
1 - I could eat a burger right now, no problem
2 - I could eat a piece of fruit right now, no problem
3 - Just stop talking about food and no one gets hurt
4 - Have you met my new best friend, the horizon?
5 - Please excuse me while I run for the railing

What do you see out the window? Draw or describe your view:

I'M ON A PLANE

Destination:

Origin:

What kind of plane are you on?

Who are you traveling with?

How early did you get up this morning?

Three words to describe how you're feeling:

How are you passing the time on the plane?

How cramped are you right now, on a scale from 1–5?
1 - I don't mean to brag, but I can feel all my extremities
2 - I've got one armrest and a super attitude
3 - Say, chaps, I don't mean to be a bother, but are we there yet?
4 - Heeeeelp
5 - Everything is numb and I can't remember feet

What do you see out the window? Draw or describe your view:

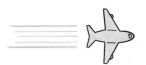

I'M ON A TRAIN

Destination:

Origin:

What kind of train are you on?

Who are you traveling with?

How early did you get up this morning?

Three words to describe how you're feeling:

How are you passing the time on the train?

How glamorous does your train travel feel right now, on a scale from 1–5?
1 - I'm just hoping to get from Point A to Point B without spelling out a four-letter word
2 - Everything's fine, but please don't tell me what that smell is
3 - This is your basic commuter train—I heard it from a really sad sandwich
4 - I'm one classy moment away from feeling like I'm in a black-and-white movie
5 - *Sips cocktail, adjusts stylish duds, stares pensively out window*

What do you see out the window? Draw or describe your view:

I'M ON A _____

(CAMEL? TUK-TUK? RICKSHAW?)

Destination:

Origin:

What kind of _____ are you on?

Who are you traveling with?

How early did you get up this morning?

Three words to describe how you're feeling:

How are you passing the time on the _____?

On a scale from 1–5, _____?
1 - _____
2 - _____
3 - _____
4 - _____
5 - _____

What do you see right now? Draw or describe your view:

MODES OF TRANSPORTATION I'VE USED WHILE TRAVELING

DATE & PLACE:

- ☐ Plane
- ☐ Train
- ☐ Boat
- ☐ Bus
- ☐ Double-decker bus
- ☐ Helicopter
- ☐ Tram
- ☐ Car
- ☐ Taxi
- ☐ Subway
- ☐ Bullet train
- ☐ Steam train
- ☐ Camper van
- ☐ Bicycle
- ☐ Moped
- ☐ Rickshaw
- ☐ Tuk-tuk
- ☐ Segway
- ☐ Scooter
- ☐ Funicular
- ☐ Aerial tramway
- ☐ Gondola
- ☐ Long-tail boat
- ☐ Rowboat
- ☐ Felucca
- ☐ Camel
- ☐ Horse
- ☐ Hot-air balloon
- ☐ Raft
- ☐ Zip line
- ☐ Sled
- ☐
- ☐
- ☐

What advice would you give to a first-time traveler?

WHICH WOULD YOU CHOOSE?

a cooking class in Thailand **OR** a pastry class in France

a ski vacation in the Alps **OR** a beach trip to Mexico

haggling at a souk in Morocco **OR** shopping in Milan

eating waffles in Belgium **OR** empanadas in Spain

rafting the Grand Canyon **OR** cycling in Yellowstone

a train trip in Europe **OR** the Trans-Siberian railway

beignets in New Orleans **OR** bagels in New York City

a safari in Kenya **OR** jungle trekking in the Amazon

Oktoberfest in Munich **OR** Lunar New Year in Beijing

a giant bowl of pho in Vietnam **OR** ramen in Japan

a trip to see Machu Picchu **OR** the Egyptian Pyramids

a lake house in Sweden **OR** a five-star hotel in London

FESTIVALS AROUND THE WORLD

What holidays and festivals have you experienced on your travels, and what were they like? Which other festivals do you want to see the most?

WISH YOU WERE HERE

Design a postcard for where you are right now. Draw the front, then choose someone to write to and compose a message on the back.

VERNAZZA
CINQUE TERRE, ITALY

AT THE BEACH

Where are you?

Who are you with?

What's the weather like?

What are you drinking?

What are the local coastal food specialties? Have you tried them yet?

When you look around, what are most of your fellow beachgoers doing? Are there a lot of families, or mostly couples and groups of friends?

What social norms do you notice, and how do they fit with your understanding of the local culture?

If you compare what you see around you to a beach scene back home, what are the primary differences?

Add a layer of sand to this jar for every beach you've visited, labeling it with the beach it represents and the dates you were there.

Write about a perfect day you had while traveling. Include as many details as possible so you can remember it forever.

BOARDING PASS
SOMEWHERE 10:15
TROPICAL C22

BOAR
SOMEWHER
TROPICAL

RIGHT PLACE, RIGHT TIME

When luck is on your side while traveling, magic happens. List and describe your best serendipitous travel moments here.

100 TRAVEL EXPERIENCES

1 _____
2 _____
3 _____
4 _____
5 _____
6 _____
7 _____
8 _____
9 _____
10 _____
11 _____
12 _____
13 _____
14 _____
15 _____
16 _____
17 _____
18 _____
19 _____
20 _____
21 _____
22 _____
23 _____
24 _____
25 _____

26 _____
27 _____
28 _____
29 _____
30 _____
31 _____
32 _____
33 _____
34 _____
35 _____
36 _____
37 _____
38 _____
39 _____
40 _____
41 _____
42 _____
43 _____
44 _____
45 _____
46 _____
47 _____
48 _____
49 _____
50 _____

I NEVER WANT TO FORGET

51 _____

52 _____

53 _____

54 _____

55 _____

56 _____

57 _____

58 _____

59 _____

60 _____

61 _____

62 _____

63 _____

64 _____

65 _____

66 _____

67 _____

68 _____

69 _____

70 _____

71 _____

72 _____

73 _____

74 _____

75 _____

76 _____

77 _____

78 _____

79 _____

80 _____

81 _____

82 _____

83 _____

84 _____

85 _____

86 _____

87 _____

88 _____

89 _____

90 _____

91 _____

92 _____

93 _____

94 _____

95 _____

96 _____

97 _____

98 _____

99 _____

100 _____

WHAT DO YOU SEE MORE CLEARLY WHEN YOU TRAVEL?

Draw or list those things inside these lenses.

Have you ever had a trip change the way you feel about something you see or interact with every day? What was it, and how did your perspective change?

_____

_____

_____

_____

_____

_____

_____

_____

_____

_____

_____

_____

_____

_____

_____

_____

_____

_____

_____

_____

_____

_____

_____

_____

H2O

QUIZ: WHAT KIND OF TRAVELER ARE YOU?

1. Which trip would you choose?
   A) Hiking and climbing Mount Kilimanjaro
   B) A street food tour of Southeast Asia
   C) NYC for Broadway, great museums, and a hugely diverse population
   D) A trip to Guatemala including a homestay with a local family

2. Which activity would you most like to do during a day of traveling?
   A) Participating in a local sport
   B) Taking a cooking class
   C) Having a coffee in a local café and people-watching
   D) A small-group tour led by a local

3. What do you think is the most essential quality or skill a traveler should have?
   A) An adventurous spirit
   B) A willingness to try anything once
   C) The ability to observe, learn, and adapt
   D) A basic command of the local language

4. What's your favorite time of day while traveling?
   A) Early morning, with bonus points for a sunrise
   B) Breakfast. No, wait—lunch. No—dinner!
   C) Whatever time of day is most active in that place
   D) Happy hour, ideally with new friends

5. What would you pack to keep yourself entertained at the beach?
   A) A surfboard
   B) A large, carefully crafted sandwich
   C) A journal and a pen
   D) A volleyball and a net

TOTAL SCORE:

GIVE YOURSELF...
1 POINT FOR EVERY A,
2 POINTS FOR EVERY B,
3 POINTS FOR EVERY C, AND
4 POINTS FOR EVERY D.

5-8 POINTS:
THE OUTDOOR ADVENTURER

As someone who enjoys both being outside and traveling, you can't resist combining the two—in fact, you're probably going to be the one who will help everyone else check off the box for "sports equipment" on their Airport Bingo pages. You know that exciting adventures make any trip more memorable, and you're a great travel companion because of it. For your next trip, consider hiking in the Swiss Alps, surfing in Hawaii, or cycling the Great Ocean Road in Australia. Happy adventuring!

9-12 POINTS:
THE EPICURE AT LARGE

For you, cultural research is best done plate by plate. You know that food is one of the best ways to get to know a place and its people, and you're adventurous enough to try it all. That openness gets you a seat at just about any table, and because great food can be found at all price points, you get to be a cultural chameleon with many different windows into the diverse levels of any culture. When planning your next trip, consider trying omakase in Japan, a wine and steak tour of Argentina, and just about anywhere and anything in Italy*Buon appetito!*

13-16 POINTS:
THE CULTURAL OBSERVER

As a keen observer and quick learner, you know that simply paying attention can get you a lot when you're traveling. You arrive having done your research, you get how to blend in upon arrival, and you leave a place with valuable understanding that many others miss— all skills that make you a huge asset to any trip. For future journeys, you are likely to enjoy both bustling cultural hubs like Amsterdam and more remote places that have been less touched by globalization, like the Mani Peninsula of Greece and a trip to Mongolia via the Trans-Mongolian railway.

17-20 POINTS:
THE PEOPLE PERSON

People are the most important piece of the cultural puzzle for you. You make friends everywhere you go, and you know that getting your boots on the ground and talking to people is one of the best possible ways to get to know a place. You're also most likely to grasp the basics of your host country's language early on (and leave with idioms and phrases you learn only by getting to know the locals). For your next trip, you'll love pub-hopping in Galway, exploring the diverse neighborhoods of Mexico City, or checking out the bustling night markets of Taipei.

BUCKET LIST: SIGHTS TO SEE

What sights from around the world do you most want to see in your lifetime?

- ☐ _____
- ☐ _____
- ☐ _____
- ☐ _____
- ☐ _____
- ☐ _____
- ☐ _____
- ☐ _____
- ☐ _____
- ☐ _____
- ☐ _____
- ☐ _____
- ☐ _____
- ☐ _____
- ☐ _____
- ☐ _____
- ☐ _____
- ☐ _____
- ☐ _____
- ☐ _____

THE TRIP OF YOUR DREAMS

IMAGINE THAT YOU COULD PLAN A TRIP WITHOUT ANY CONSTRAINTS ON BUDGET OR LOGISTICS. WHAT WOULD YOUR TRIP OF A LIFETIME LOOK LIKE?

Where would you go?

Who would you go with?

What sights would you see?

Where would you stay?

What would you do while you were there?

What would you eat and drink?

What would you wear?

OPTIONAL: Come back down to earth for a second. Are there any aspects of this trip you could actually pull off? What would it take to make it happen? You might find that with a little planning, saving, and travel smarts, you can make some version of this dream a reality.

PARIS IS NOT A CITY; IT'S A WORLD.
—KING FRANCIS I

STREET FASHION

From the effortless chic of Paris to Tokyo's bold streetwear, fashion is a great window into a culture. Draw or describe the trends and unique pieces you've seen around the world.

AT THE CAFÉ

Where are you?

Who are you with?

What are you drinking?

What are the local coffee or tea specialties? Have you tried them yet?

When you look around, what are the other people in the café doing? Are they mostly alone or in groups?

What social norms do you notice, and how do they fit with your understanding of the local culture?

If you compare what you see around you to a café back home, what are the primary differences?

DRINKS WITH A VIEW

Whether it's hot-cocoa-with-mountains-in-the-background spectacular or just your usual cup of coffee in a new setting, the chance to sip and take it all in slowly is one of the traveler's greatest joys. Draw what you're drinking and what your view is, and record the date and location to better preserve your memory.

THE MOST MEMORABLE PEOPLE I'VE MET ON MY TRAVELS

¡Encantado de conocerte!

What do you want locals to feel or know about people from your country? How can you make sure you represent it well?

_____

_____

_____

_____

_____

_____

_____

_____

_____

_____

_____

_____

_____

_____

_____

_____

_____

_____

_____

_____

_____

_____

_____

_____

_____

FIVE SENSES

As you explore, record your observations of what each place smells like, tastes like, feels like, sounds like, and looks like in the chart below.

PLACE	SENSORY OBSERVATIONS

WORLD SANDWICH CHECKLIST

date and location:

- ☐ Banh mi
- ☐ *Torta*
- ☐ Philly cheesesteak
- ☐ Croque monsieur
- ☐ Bombay sandwich
- ☐ *Kaya* toast
- ☐ *Bocadillo"*
- ☐ *Katsu sando*
- ☐ *Francesinha*
- ☐ Porchetta panino
- ☐ *Medianoche*
- ☐ Nashville hot chicken sandwich
- ☐ Gatsby sandwich
- ☐ Po'boy
- ☐ Mallorca
- ☐
- ☐
- ☐

(Vegetarian? Try these: Italian mozzarella in *carrozza*, Indian *vada pav*, English cucumber sandwiches, American grilled cheese, Senegalese bean sandwiches, Israeli *sabich*, and—sorry not sorry—Australian Vegemite sandwiches!)

Who are your favorite travel companions and why?

ROAD TRIP

Ahhh, the open road. Use this page to document an epic road trip!

START AND END DATE:

DRAW OR TAPE IN YOUR ROUTE HERE:

FELLOW ROAD TRIPPERS:

VEHICLE:

TOTAL MILES DRIVEN:

FAVORITE SNACKS EATEN:

BEST MEALS HAD:

INSIDE JOKES FROM THE TRIP:

ROAD TRIP PLAYLIST:

REMEMBER WHEN _____

_____

_____

_____

_____?

WE COULDN'T HAVE DONE IT WITHOUT:

I'LL NEVER LOOK AT _____ THE SAME WAY

ALL-TIME BEST TRIP QUOTES

Fill this page with the best quotes from you and your travel companions, plus when and where they were said.

I either just paid for our gas or I gave a random stranger twenty euros.
—The author's husband, Italy, 2015

A ROOM WITH A VIEW

DRAW WHAT YOU SEE OUT THE WINDOW WHERE YOU'RE STAYING

THE MOST MEMORABLE PLACES I'VE STAYED

Sometimes a place to stay is memorable because it's amazing, and sometimes it's memorable because you've seen things you can't unsee. From the incredible to the less-than-ideal, list and describe the most unique places where you've stayed.

Imagine how your life would be different if you lived in one of the places you've visited. What would your typical day look like? What would you eat? What would be different about your life there, and what would be the same?

_____

_____

_____

_____

_____

_____

_____

_____

_____

_____

_____

_____

_____

_____

_____

_____

_____

_____

_____

_____

_____

_____

DRAW YOUR DREAM LIVING SPACE FOR THE ALTERNATE LIFE YOU JUST DESCRIBED

FROM MOROCCO TO MEXICO, BEAUTIFUL TILEWORK AND MOSAICS CAN BE FOUND ALL OVER THE WORLD. USE THE SQUARES ON THIS PAGE TO RE-CREATE AND COLOR IN TILE PATTERNS YOU SEE ON YOUR TRAVELS.

LOCAL COLOR

Have you ever noticed that different places have distinct color palettes? Add colors to the paint palettes below to represent the color schemes of places you've been.

PLACE: _____

PLACE: _____

PLACE: _____

PLACE: _____

PLACE: _____

PLACE: _____

PLACE: _____

PLACE: _____

PLACE: _____

QUIZ: WHICH CASTLE OR PALACE SHOULD YOU VISIT?

1. What's your number one castle goal?
   A) Ghosts or it didn't happen
   B) Being tipsy on some of the world's best beer
   C) I just want to be surrounded by shiny things
   D) Great snacks after the exploring is complete

2. What kind of weather would you prefer?
   A) Misty and spooky, please and thank you
   B) It doesn't matter as long as I feel like I'm in a damn fairy tale
   C) Hot with a side of noodles
   D) Hot with a side of curry

3. What would you like to do after you're done seeing the castle?
   A) Pub it up with my mates
   B) Cozy up with some hot booze at a Christmas market
   C) Shop and snack my way through a night market
   D) Eat until I'm made out of naan

4. What kind of castle history interests you the most?
   A) A fortress, a prison, and some creepy stories
   B) The life story of a single very unusual person
   C) Your usual palace classics: royalty, ceremony, and tradition
   D) Fascinating architecture and gender history

5. What color do you want the castle to be?
   A) The kind of gray that could be labeled as "old castle color" in a crayon box
   B) White and straight out of a Disney movie, please!
   C) Why choose one color when you can have them ALL?
   D) Pink! Pink! Pink!

TOTAL SCORE:

GIVE YOURSELF...
1 POINT FOR EVERY A,
2 POINTS FOR EVERY B,
3 POINTS FOR EVERY C, AND
4 POINTS FOR EVERY D.

5-8 POINTS:
EDINBURGH CASTLE
EDINBURGH, SCOTLAND

If you're in search of a classic castle experience, look no further. Historic Edinburgh Castle is thought to be one of the most haunted places in Scotland. While you're there, take a tour of the dungeons and hear about the reported ghost sightings in the castle's 900-year history. You might also see if any of the historical reenactments at the castle will coincide with your visit, and do consider a visit to the traditional tea room for scones with clotted cream. Just remember—even if you get spooked, keep the heid!

9-12 POINTS:
NEUSCHWANSTEIN CASTLE
BAVARIA, GERMANY

A stunning castle with a dark history, lovely Neuschwanstein Castle has it all: fairy-tale architecture, a fascinating backstory, and loads of intrigue. Built for King Ludwig II of Bavaria, who was alternately called the "Fairy-Tale King" and "Mad King Ludwig," the castle's history is well worth a read for all its twists and turns. With the nearest town nestled right at the foot of the Alps and the fact that the whole region is known for some of the world's best beer and comfort food, you should probably just start packing a bag now. *Gute Reise!*

13-16 POINTS:
THE GRAND PALACE
BANGKOK, THAILAND

One of the most iconic palaces in the world, Bangkok's Grand Palace and its surrounding complex is a must-see. With ornate patterns in shiny gold, rich color, and mirrored tiles, the buildings in the complex are some of the most jaw-dropping structures in the world, and the palace itself is an important site for tradition and ceremony in Thailand. And after exploring the grounds, you will have definitely earned yourself a cold Thai iced tea and a massive bowl of *pad see ew*. And some papaya salad. And a few pieces of roti ... and mango sticky rice ...

17-20 POINTS:
HAWA MAHAL
JAIPUR, INDIA

Also known as the "Pink Palace," Hawa Mahal is one of the most beautiful palaces in the world. Gorgeous in color and built with a unique honeycomb design, the palace is world-famous for its architecture, which also has some really interesting history behind it. As an added bonus, the local cuisine is spectacular, with lots of spicy, sweet, and deep-fried delights waiting to be sampled before and after your visit to the palace. Grab a lassi if it's hot, and don't miss *pyaz kachori*, a fried pastry street food snack that's a local favorite.

MY FAVORITE CITIES IN THE WORLD

Out of all the cities to choose from, which are your favorites so far? (You may want to use pencil for this page—the list is bound to change and grow over time!)

CITY OF DREAMS

Pick and choose elements of your favorite real cities
to create your ultimate imaginary city below.

MY DREAM CITY WOULD HAVE:

The architecture of _____

The food of _____

The fashion of _____

The arts culture of _____

Lots of _____

And no _____

A statue of _____

A museum dedicated to _____

A strong tradition of _____

A thriving population of wild _____

And a world-famous _____

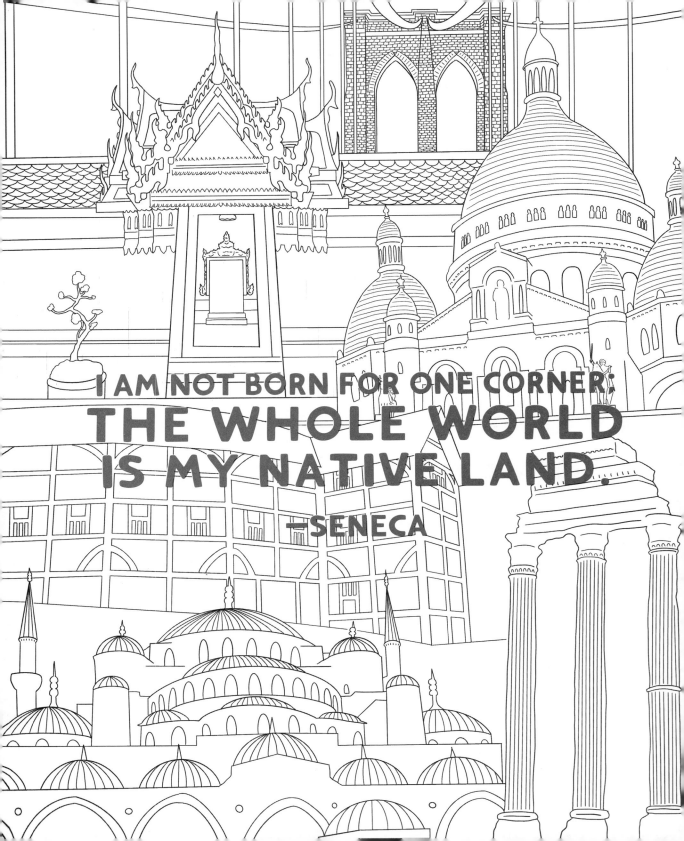

Write about a place you've been whose culture inspires you. What makes it special? Does it make you want to change anything in your own life?

PASSPORT

FINDING YOUR WAY IN

Before your next big trip, use this page to help you research how to understand and immerse yourself in the local culture while you're there. Then, use the questions on the opposite page to reflect on the experience in real time.

ESSENTIAL LANGUAGE PHRASES:

MOST IMPORTANT RULES OF ETIQUETTE:

HISTORY TO KNOW ABOUT:

CURRENT ISSUES AND POLITICAL CLIMATE:

OFF-THE-BEATEN-PATH PLACES TO SEE:

BEST PUBLIC TRANSIT OPTIONS AND WALKING ROUTES:

TYPICAL DAILY SCHEDULE:

DAYS/TIMES WHEN THINGS WILL BE CLOSED:

WHERE DO LOCALS HANG OUT? ARE THERE PLACES NEAR WHERE YOU'RE STAYING THAT ARE CENTRAL TO DAILY LIFE?

QUESTIONS FOR WHILE YOU'RE ON THE GROUND

WHAT STRATEGIES ARE WORKING FOR CULTURAL IMMERSION SO FAR? WHAT STRATEGIES AREN'T WORKING?

WHAT HAVE YOU OBSERVED THAT YOU MIGHT NOT HAVE NOTICED IF YOU HADN'T DONE YOUR RESEARCH AHEAD OF TIME?

WHAT HAVE YOU SEEN THAT RESONATES WITH YOU MOST?

ARE THERE THINGS YOU'VE FOUND CONFUSING?

CAN YOU TRACE YOUR REACTIONS TO BOTH THE POSITIVE AND THE PUZZLING BACK TO YOUR OWN CULTURE'S VALUES AND NORMS?

WHAT DO YOU THINK A TRAVELER'S RESPONSIBILITIES ARE WHEN INTERACTING WITH LOCALS? HOW ARE YOU UPHOLDING THOSE RESPONSIBILITIES SO FAR?

OTHER NOTES:

BOOK A TRIP

For those excruciating waits in between trips, travel reads can be your best friends. List the best travel-related books you've read—and the ones you want to check off your list—here.

With the pressures of social media and the constant presence of technology, how can you stay authentic while traveling? Brainstorm ways to stay in the moment and still share your experiences in a way that feels true to who you are.

SLIGHTLY LONGERGRAMS

Snapping a photo only takes a second, but drawing something forces you to slow down; and while social media allows us to share our travel experiences, there's something to be said for the moments you get to keep for yourself. In the squares below, focus on something you would normally have Instagrammed and draw it instead.

FLYING SOLO

Sometimes, traveling alone allows us to see things we would have otherwise missed. Use this page to either plan your ideal solo trip or document a trip you went on by yourself.

Un tavolo per uno, per favore.

What are the biggest things you've learned about yourself while traveling?

_____
_____
_____
_____
_____
_____
_____
_____
_____
_____
_____
_____
_____
_____
_____
_____
_____
_____
_____
_____
_____
_____
_____
_____
_____
_____
_____

THE EARLIEST I'VE EVER SET AN ALARM FOR A FLIGHT:

THE LATEST I'VE EVER STAYED UP WHILE TRAVELING:

THE LONGEST I'VE SPENT IN TRANSIT:

THE BIGGEST CITY I'VE BEEN TO:

THE OLDEST LANDMARK OR RUIN I'VE SEEN:

THE FARTHEST DISTANCE I'VE TRAVELED FROM HOME:

THE MOST STEPS I'VE WALKED IN A DAY WHILE TRAVELING:

THE HOTTEST PLACE I'VE BEEN TO:

THE COLDEST PLACE I'VE BEEN TO:

THE MOST ADVENTUROUS THING I'VE DONE WHILE TRAVELING:

THE MOST SPONTANEOUS TRIP I'VE EVER TAKEN:

THE MOST HILARIOUS TRAVEL FAIL I'VE HAD:

THE CRAZIEST TWENTY-FOUR HOURS I'VE HAD WHILE TRAVELING:

THE MOST EPIC TRAVEL EXPERIENCE I'VE HAD:

THE MOST HILARIOUS FOREIGN-LANGUAGE MISHAP I'VE HAD:

THE MOST CHALLENGING THING I'VE DONE WHILE TRAVELING:

THE MOST LIFE-CHANGING TRAVEL EXPERIENCE I'VE HAD:

WHAT I'M MOST PROUD OF HAVING DONE ON MY TRAVELS:

WORLD DUMPLING CHECKLIST

date and location:

- ☐ *Momo*
- ☐ Samosa
- ☐ *Manti*
- ☐ *Gyoza*
- ☐ *Khinkali*
- ☐ Knish
- ☐ *Shumai*
- ☐ Agnolotti
- ☐ Pierogi
- ☐ *Mandu*
- ☐ Matzo ball
- ☐ Gnocchi
- ☐ Chicken and dumplings
- ☐ Pelmeni
- ☐ *Xiaolongbao*
- ☐
- ☐
- ☐

(Vegetarian? Many of the dumplings on this list commonly come with a vegetarian filling option, but you can also try these alternatives: ricotta ravioli, vegetable *baozi*, potato *kreplach*, mushroom *uszka*, and *modak*.)

SNACK CRAWL > PUB CRAWL

Who needs a full meal when you can spend an afternoon, an evening, or an entire day sampling incredible snacks and small plates from all over a city? Plan the perfect snack crawl, and draw or describe your best bites from the experience.

BUCKET LIST: GLOBAL EATS

Which foods from around the world do you most want to sample at the source?

- [ ] _____
- [ ] _____
- [ ] _____
- [ ] _____
- [ ] _____
- [ ] _____
- [ ] _____
- [ ] _____
- [ ] _____
- [ ] _____
- [ ] _____
- [ ] _____
- [ ] _____
- [ ] _____
- [ ] _____
- [ ] _____
- [ ] _____
- [ ] _____

Describe how you feel while you're traveling. Do different sides of your personality show up? Which ones, and how?

_____

_____

_____

_____

_____

_____

_____

_____

_____

_____

_____

_____

_____

_____

_____

_____

_____

_____

_____

_____

_____

_____

_____

_____

PORTRAIT OF A TRAVELER

**IMAGINE YOU'RE MIDWAY THROUGH AN EPIC JOURNEY.
DRAW THE SELF-PORTRAIT YOU'D SEE REFLECTED BACK AT YOU.**

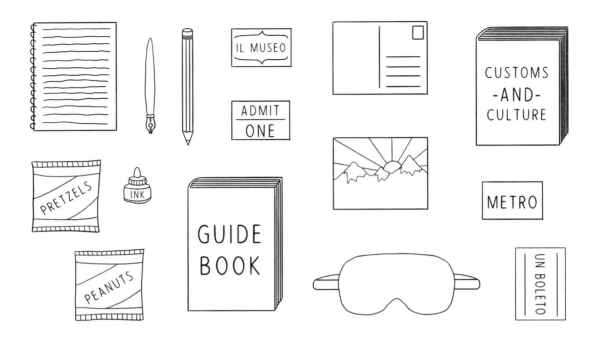

ONCE THE TRAVEL BUG BITES THERE IS NO KNOWN ANTIDOTE, AND I KNOW THAT I SHALL BE HAPPILY INFECTED UNTIL THE END OF MY LIFE.
— MICHAEL PALIN

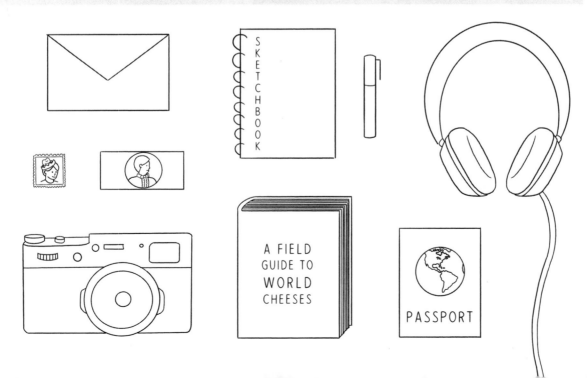

I NEVER UNDERSTOOD _____ UNTIL
I TRAVELED TO _____

MY TRIP TO _____ TAUGHT ME
HOW TO _____

GOING TO _____ MADE ME WANT TO
LEARN MORE ABOUT _____

IF I HADN'T TRAVELED TO _____, I NEVER
WOULD HAVE _____

SEEING _____ INSPIRED ME TO
TRY _____

I DIDN'T KNOW I _____ UNTIL
I WENT TO _____

BEING IN _____ LED ME TO
DISCOVER _____

TRAVELING TO _____ GAVE ME A NEW
PERSPECTIVE ON _____

LEARNING HOW TO _____ WAS
THE BEST PART OF TRAVELING TO _____

I DIDN'T KNOW THE MEANING OF _____ UNTIL I
EXPERIENCED _____

Write about the most culturally baffling moment you've experienced while traveling. Can you better understand it when you look back on it now? What would you do differently next time?

_____

_____

_____

_____

_____

_____

_____

_____

_____

_____

_____

_____

_____

_____

_____

_____

_____

_____

_____

_____

THERE'S A WORD FOR THAT

In Icelandic, *ísbíltúr* means "a road trip to get ice cream." (Yes, please!)
Use this page to record the most interesting and untranslatable words
you've come across in your travels and reading.

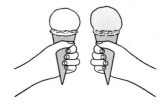

DIGGING DEEPER

Sometimes, the things we see or learn about a place clash with our own understanding of how the world works—and when that happens, the best thing a traveler can do is dig deeper. List questions and observations on this page, then record the insights you gain after getting to know a place better. Use the questions on the opposite page as a guide to getting curious and achieving that deeper understanding.

WHAT'S DIFFERENT ABOUT THIS CULTURE FROM YOUR OWN? WHAT CAN YOU LEARN FROM THE CONTRAST?

WHAT SOCIAL NORMS AND ETIQUETTE RULES ARE IMPORTANT HERE? WHAT CAN YOU FIGURE OUT ABOUT THIS CULTURE FROM THOSE GUIDELINES?

TAKE A LOOK AT THIS PLACE'S BIGGEST HOLIDAYS, TRADITIONS, AND FESTIVALS. DO THEY TELL YOU ANYTHING ABOUT WHAT HAS TRADITIONALLY BEEN IMPORTANT HERE?

DO YOU KNOW OF ANY MAJOR HISTORICAL EVENTS THAT HAVE CONTRIBUTED TO THIS CULTURE'S WORLDVIEW AND WAY OF LIFE?

SOME CULTURES ARE MORE INDIVIDUALISTIC, WHILE OTHERS ARE COLLECTIVIST. WHICH BETTER DESCRIBES THE PLACE YOU'RE RESEARCHING?

WHEN YOU TAKE ALL THESE FACTORS INTO CONSIDERATION, CAN YOU IDENTIFY PATTERNS THAT MIGHT TELL YOU MORE ABOUT WHAT THE CENTRAL VALUES OF THIS CULTURE ARE?

WHEN YOU APPLY THAT UNDERSTANDING TO YOUR QUESTIONS, WHAT HAPPENS? CAN YOU PUT WHAT YOU WERE CURIOUS ABOUT INTO CONTEXT?

THERE'S NO COW ON THE ICE

That's the translation of a Swedish idiom used to mean "Don't worry."
Fill in these quote bubbles with idioms you've learned on your travels
(bonus points if you learn them from locals!).

GLOBETROTTER
CHALLENGE
LEVEL 2

- ☐ Go somewhere that requires getting a visa

- ☐ Have a friendly conversation with a local in their language

- ☐ Read a book in the place it was written

- ☐ Stay, dine, and shop small and local for an entire trip

- ☐ Participate in a major festival in another country

- ☐ Go back to a destination for a second time

THE SECOND TIME AROUND

Though traveling somewhere new is always exciting, each trip back to a place you've already visited helps you peel away its layers and gain a richer understanding. Where would you like to go back to, and why?

Bon retour!

Write about the second trip you took to a place you'd already been. How was it different this time around? Would you go back a third time—and, if so, what would you do differently?

WELCOME
BACK!

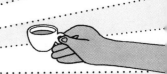

PLACES I'VE SEEN THE SUNRISE

PLACES I'VE SEEN THE SUNSET

IT'S THE LITTLE THINGS

From real New England maple syrup to a steaming mug of tea in Sri Lanka, small pleasures await us all over the world. List or draw the best little joys you've experienced on your travels.

Across the world, different cultures have varying definitions of what "the good life" looks like. What's your definition, and how does it compare to what you've seen on your travels?

_____

_____

_____

_____

_____

_____

_____

_____

_____

_____

_____

_____

_____

_____

_____

_____

_____

_____

_____

_____

_____

THE ABCS OF MY
ADVENTURES

A
B
C
D
E
F
G
H
I
J
K
L
M

FILL IN EACH LETTER WITH SOMETHING YOU'VE EXPERIENCED ON YOUR TRAVELS

N

O

P

Q

R

S

T

U

V

W

X

Y

Z

STUFFED, SUNBURNED & SMILING

Fill in the name of a place you've visited in the leftmost blank,
then choose three words to describe how you felt there.

_____ : _____ + _____ + _____

_____ : _____ + _____ + _____

_____ : _____ + _____ + _____

_____ : _____ + _____ + _____

_____ : _____ + _____ + _____

_____ : _____ + _____ + _____

_____ : _____ + _____ + _____

_____ : _____ + _____ + _____

_____ : _____ + _____ + _____

_____ : _____ + _____ + _____

Write about the trips that have had the most profound impact on who you are today. What made them so significant? How do you feel looking back on them now?

_____

_____

_____

_____

_____

_____

_____

_____

_____

_____

_____

_____

_____

_____

_____

_____

_____

_____

_____

_____

_____

_____

_____

_____

_____

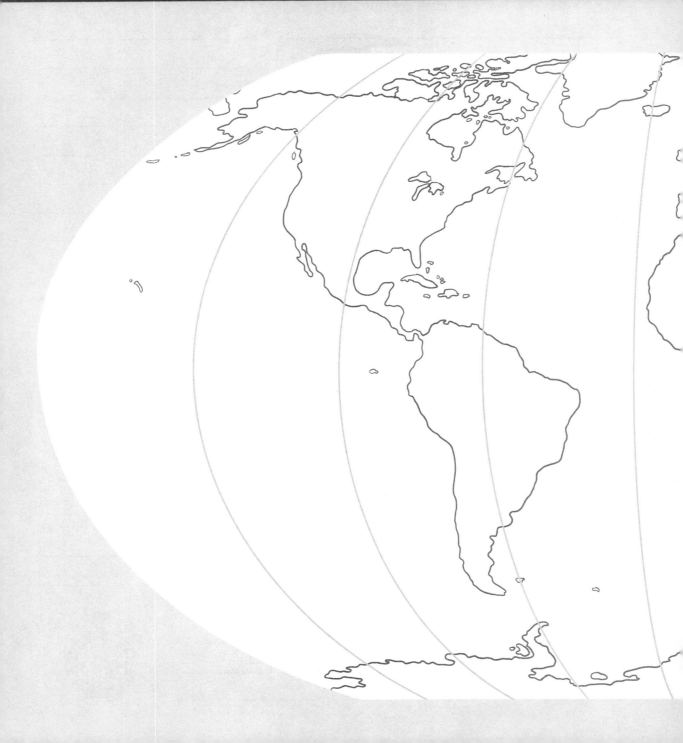

PLANELY STRANGE

Air travel creates some of the funniest and most bizarre situations out there. What are the oddest things you've ever seen happen on a plane?

Excuse me? My chicken doesn't seem to have any chicken in it.

AT THE STATION

Where are you?

Where are you going today, with which form of transportation?

Who are you with?

How did you buy your ticket, and how much did it cost?

When you look around, what are most of your fellow passengers doing while they wait? Are they vacationers or locals? Do they appear to be traveling for business or leisure?

What social norms do you notice, and how do they fit with your understanding of the local culture?

If you compare what you see around you to a transit station back home, what are the primary differences?

PUT YOUR STAMP ON IT

What would passport stamps look like if you designed them? Fill this page with stamps for places you've been or places you're dying to visit.

VISAS

Visit the countryside or a village while traveling, then write about the experience. What did you see that you might have missed if you had stayed in the city?

_____

_____

_____

_____

_____

_____

_____

_____

_____

_____

_____

_____

_____

_____

_____

_____

_____

_____

_____

_____

_____

HOW CAN YOU BECOME AN EVEN MORE MINDFUL TRAVELER?
CONSIDER THE WAYS YOU CAN ACHIEVE THIS IDEAL THROUGH
THE DAILY CHOICES YOU MAKE WHILE TRAVELING.

SLOW DOWN

KEEP AN OPEN MIND

MAKE CONSCIOUS CHOICES

QUIZ: WHICH OFF-THE-BEATEN-PATH PLACE SHOULD YOU VISIT NEXT?

1. How remote is too remote?
    A. Let's just say I'm a big fan of civilization.
    B. I like to use a city as a base and explore from there.
    C. Let's bushwhack! But can we stay in a nice, eco-friendly lodge?
    D. I'd go to the ends of the earth for the adventure of a lifetime!

2. Which food experience do you most want to try?
    A. Rice pilaf scooped from the biggest cauldron you've ever seen in your life
    B. A progression of different dishes fresh off the grill
    C. A traditional stew cooked low and slow in a cast-iron pot over a wood fire
    D. A squeaky cheese, served hot and toasty

3. Which landscape would you most want to explore?
    A. A real desert, complete with dunes and ancient history
    B. Diverse scenery is a plus, but beaches are a must
    C. Lush wetlands filled with wildlife
    D. A golden-lit arctic forest

4. Which animal would you be most excited to see in the wild?
    A. A saiga antelope
    B. A capybara
    C. An elephant
    D. A reindeer

5. Which experience appeals to you most?
    A. Exploring an ancient city written about by the world's most famous explorers
    B. Chilling on the beach and eating grilled meats
    C. Witnessing a massive animal migration in a way that doesn't interfere with it
    D. Seeing the northern lights from behind a sled

TOTAL SCORE:

GIVE YOURSELF...
1 POINT FOR EVERY A,
2 POINTS FOR EVERY B,
3 POINTS FOR EVERY C, AND
4 POINTS FOR EVERY D.

5-8 POINTS:
UZBEKISTAN

Ancient cities, Silk Road history, and a culture with a worldwide reputation for hospitality are just some of the amazing things you'll find in Uzbekistan. Packed with sights including mosques, bazaars, mausoleums, silk workshops, and more, this gem of Central Asia is a showstopper for anyone interested in ancient cultures—and is cropping up on more and more lists of up-and-coming travel destinations. While there, don't miss Samarkand—an ancient city founded in the 7th century BCE and called the "Crossroad of Cultures"— and be sure to sample *plov,* a traditional rice pilaf cooked in gigantic cauldrons and served in large portions.

9-12 POINTS:
URUGUAY

Beaches, bustling city life, hot springs, and a hopping *Carnaval*—Uruguay has it all, served up alongside a massive platter of grilled meats. South America's smallest country has a lot to offer, and now is a great time to go. This country has seen fewer tourists than some of its neighbors, but has just as much charm, and is starting to attract more attention with good reason. For a taste of vibrant city life and a great arts scene, check out the capital city of Montevideo; to unwind, head to the coast, where gorgeous beaches await; and to fuel your adventures, get yourself a churro (or twelve) with dulce de leche.

13-16 POINTS:
BOTSWANA

Have you always wanted to go on a safari but find yourself wary of the environmental impact? Botswana is the destination for you. Because it has purposefully shunned mass tourism and made careful choices to encourage environmental protection and conscientious travel, the unique quality of experiences awaiting travelers who make the trek to this African nation is unparalleled. Don't miss Chobe National Park—home to the world's largest elephant herds—and the famous Okavango Delta, which offers some of the most spectacular wildlife viewing in the world. This is wilderness at its finest, and a perfect choice for the ethically minded traveler.

17-20 POINTS:
SÁPMI (OTHERWISE KNOWN AS LAPLAND)

If you look up "off the beaten path" in a dictionary, you might just see Lapland listed as the definition. This vast area occupying the northern parts of Finland, Sweden, Norway, and into Russia is a paradise for anyone who wants to truly get away from it all. Sparsely populated, remote, and breathtakingly beautiful, the area is best explored by ski or sled, with excellent hiking opportunities as well. And depending on the season, you might have a chance to catch a glimpse of the northern lights or experience twenty-four-hour daylight (all the more time for snacking on Leipäjuusto—that toasty Finnish cheese!).

FAVORITE CHEAP EATS

Featuring all-stars like bakery pastries, street-food snacks, and a vast and diverse landscape of international sandwiches, the realm of low-budget bites is one of the best culinary worlds to explore while traveling. Draw or list the best cheap eats you've had on your travels.

WORLD NOODLE & PASTA CHECKLIST

date and location:

- ☐ *Cacio e pepe*
- ☐ Ramen
- ☐ *Pad kee mao*
- ☐ *Fideo*
- ☐ Pho
- ☐ Couscous
- ☐ *Japchae*
- ☐ *Sorrentinos*
- ☐ *Cheung fun*
- ☐ Pastitsio
- ☐ Spätzle
- ☐ *Dan dan* noodles
- ☐ *Laksa*
- ☐ Lasagne alla Bolognese
- ☐ *Kushari*
- ☐
- ☐
- ☐

(Vegetarian? Many of the above are too, but you can always substitute these alternatives: Japanese soba noodles, *Thai pad woon sen*, Chinese chow mein, Peruvian *tallarines*, or Korean *bibim guksu*.)

OH, THE THINGS I'VE EATEN DEEP FRIED

There are many things that unite us as a species, no matter where we're from—and the tradition of deep frying is one of them. Use this page to list everything you've eaten deep-fried on your travels.

ADVENTURES IN EATING

I DIDN'T KNOW
WHAT THIS WAS
WHEN I ATE IT

THIS WAS
SURPRISINGLY
TASTY

THIS WAS VISUALLY
CHALLENGING BUT
DELICIOUS

THIS IS SOMETHING
I ATE TO BE POLITE

THIS IS SOMETHING I
ATE THINKING IT WAS
SOMETHING ELSE

I NEVER SAW THIS
FILLING COMING

DON'T TELL MY
MOM I ATE THIS

THIS IS A FRUIT/VEGETABLE
I HAD NEVER SEEN BEFORE

F FOR NUTRITION,
A+ FOR TASTE

Travel often teaches us about our own way of life more than we expect. What has traveling to other places taught you about your own culture?

_____
_____
_____
_____
_____
_____
_____
_____
_____
_____
_____
_____
_____
_____
_____
_____
_____
_____
_____
_____
_____
_____
_____
_____
_____

YOU KNOW THOSE TIMES WHEN EVERYTHING GOES WRONG AND ALL YOU CAN DO IS LAUGH? TAKE ONE OF YOUR MOST HILARIOUS TRAVEL MISADVENTURES AND PRETEND IT'S BEING MADE INTO A MOVIE.

TITLE AND TAGLINE:

STARRING:

RATING:

SOUNDTRACK:

DESCRIBE OR DRAW KEY SCENES FROM THE TRAILER:

MOVIE POSTER:

LOST IN MISTRANSLATION

What are the most hilarious mistranslations and language misunderstandings you've encountered on your travels?

I believe that's supposed to be CRAB salad. With a B.

While traveling, spend a day consciously trying to listen more and talk less. What did you hear and what did you notice?

_____
_____
_____
_____
_____
_____
_____
_____
_____
_____
_____
_____
_____
_____
_____
_____
_____
_____
_____
_____
_____
_____
_____
_____
_____

THE WORD ON THE STREET

List the best insider tips and recommendations you've gotten from locals.

THIS BAR IS ACTUALLY A
SECRET JAZZ CLUB
FROM MIDNIGHT UNTIL
THE TIME YOU USUALLY
GO TO WORK BACK HOME

AT THE MARKET

Where are you?

Who are you with?

What kinds of goods are being sold at the different stalls? What do you see that you wouldn't find in a market back home?

Are the other shoppers mostly alone or are they there with friends or family? Are they fellow travelers or locals?

When you look around, what's the general mood at the market? Is it leisurely and slow-paced, or busy and chaotic?

What social norms do you notice, and how do they fit with your understanding of the local culture?

If you compare what you see around you to a market back home, what are the primary differences?

THE WHOLE WISE WORLD

Fill this page with proverbs, quotes, and other bits of wisdom
you encounter from different cultures on your travels.

Madagascan
Owl

African
Grass Owl

Sri Lanka
Bay Owl

Eurasian
Eagle Owl

While traveling, find a bench or other place to sit and fill this page with a stream-of-consciousness description of everything you see.

UNDER THE SURFACE

Every culture is like an iceberg: there are parts you can see, and there's a lot happening below the surface. Pick a place you've visited and fill the top of the iceberg with the visible components of its culture, like fashion, food, and festivals. Then, fill the area under the surface with social norms, abstract values, and anything else you perceive that isn't visible. As an optional bonus step, draw lines between anything you can connect on the two different levels.

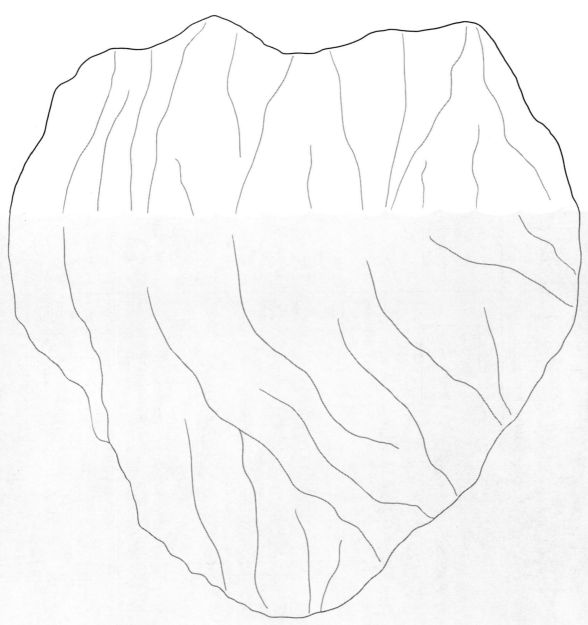

Reflect on how privilege and cultural appropriation affect how we interact with other communities. What are your feelings on this topic, and what does being a good global citizen mean to you?

_____
_____
_____
_____
_____
_____
_____
_____
_____
_____
_____
_____
_____
_____
_____
_____
_____
_____
_____
_____
_____
_____

LISTEN & LEARN

AT THE PARK

Where are you?

Who are you with?

Are the other people around you mostly alone or are they there with friends or family? Are they fellow travelers or locals?

When you look around, what are people doing? Are they playing a sport, having a picnic, reading, or chatting with their friends or family?

What social norms do you notice, and how do they fit with your understanding of the local culture?

If you compare what you see around you to a park back home, what are the primary differences?

QUE FLORA FLORA

When you travel to a different climate, you often see different plants and flowers from what you see every day back home. Draw or describe some memorable ones and list where you saw them.

FOR THE FAUNA IT

List or draw the animal species you've seen in the wild on your travels, noting when and where each sighting took place.

BUCKET LIST: EPIC EXPERIENCES

From gorilla-spotting in Rwanda to skydiving in New Zealand, what thrilling adventures do you most want to have around the world?

- [ ] _____
- [ ] _____
- [ ] _____
- [ ] _____
- [ ] _____
- [ ] _____
- [ ] _____
- [ ] _____
- [ ] _____
- [ ] _____
- [ ] _____
- [ ] _____
- [ ] _____
- [ ] _____
- [ ] _____
- [ ] _____
- [ ] _____
- [ ] _____
- [ ] _____

What fears have you faced while traveling? Reflect on those experiences below. What did you learn from confronting your fear?

_____

_____

_____

_____

_____

_____

_____

_____

_____

_____

_____

_____

_____

_____

_____

_____

_____

_____

_____

_____

_____

_____

_____

_____

_____

THOUGH WE TRAVEL THE WORLD OVER TO FIND THE BEAUTIFUL, WE MUST CARRY IT WITH US OR WE FIND IT NOT.

— RALPH WALDO EMERSON

Purposefully unplug for an hour, afternoon, day, or more while you're away, then write about how it went. What was it like? Did you gain any insights from the experience?

_____

_____

_____

_____

_____

_____

_____

_____

_____

_____

_____

_____

_____

_____

_____

_____

_____

_____

_____

_____

_____

_____

_____

_____

RIGHT ON SCHEDULE

Having dinner at nine p.m. might sound crazy depending on where you're from, but your best bet for truly experiencing local culture is to put yourself on the schedule of the place you're in. Write in your normal schedule back home on the left, then use the column on the right to record what you did on local time in one of your favorite far-flung locales.

A DAY BACK HOME

A DAY IN _____

HOUR BY HOUR

An early-morning swim, a nightcap in a crazy thunderstorm, or maybe just a most unwelcome wake-up call for a ridiculously early flight—travel adventures occur at all hours. For each hour of the day, list something memorable, epic, or unusual you did on your travels at that time somewhere around the world.

05:00 _____

06:00 _____

07:00 _____

08:00 _____

09:00 _____

10:00 _____

11:00 _____

12:00 _____

13:00 _____

14:00 _____

15:00 _____

16:00 _____

17:00 _____

18:00 _____

19:00 _____

20:00 _____

21:00 _____

22:00 _____

23:00 _____

00:00 _____

01:00 _____

02:00 _____

03:00 _____

04:00 _____

IF YOU COULD BE ANYWHERE IN THE WORLD RIGHT NOW, WHERE WOULD YOU CHOOSE? DRAW WHERE YOU'D LIKE TO BE AND WHAT YOU'D BE DOING.

Often, we return from a trip with a renewed sense of clarity and inspiration for our own lives. Use this page to explore those feelings. What did you realize about your own life from this experience? Are there any changes you hope to make?

_____

_____

_____

_____

_____

_____

_____

_____

_____

_____

_____

_____

_____

_____

_____

_____

_____

_____

_____

_____

_____

_____

_____

MOST MEMORABLE MEALS

Some of our best travel memories take place around the table. Draw, describe, or list the most memorable meals from your travels.

WORLD DESSERT CHECKLIST

date and location:

- [ ] Baklava
- [ ] Mochi
- [ ] *Apfelstrudel*
- [ ] *Brigadeiro*
- [ ] Shave ice
- [ ] Tiramisu
- [ ] Sticky toffee pudding
- [ ] *Alfajor*
- [ ] *Pastel de nata*
- [ ] Mango sticky rice
- [ ] *Gulab jamun*
- [ ] Halvah
- [ ] Belgian waffle
- [ ] Nanaimo bar
- [ ] Tres leches cake
- [ ]
- [ ]
- [ ]

DO TRY THIS AT HOME

Find a recipe for a local dish you loved from your travels. Be sure to note (or bring back!) any specialty ingredients you'll need to re-create it as closely as possible.

INGREDIENTS

DIRECTIONS

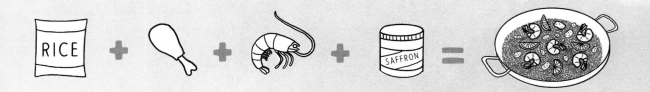

THAT CERTAIN SOMETHING

Saffron in Iran, dill in Scandinavia, and harissa in Tunisia—what ingredients make each cuisine taste the way it does? Fill in the table below with the central ingredients used in each place and its most iconic dishes.

PLACE	INGREDIENTS	DISHES

GIVE THANKS

From how fast we're able to cross long distances to the fact that traveling is possible only because another community is opening its doors to you, there's a lot of room for gratitude in the world of travel. Fill this page with everything you're grateful for as a traveler.

Write about a single moment you had while traveling that made you feel a strong sense of gratitude.

_____

_____

_____

_____

_____

_____

_____

_____

_____

_____

_____

_____

_____

_____

_____

_____

_____

_____

_____

_____

_____

_____

_____

_____

IF YOU COULD SEND A FRIEND ON THEIR DREAM VACATION, WITH NO RESTRICTIONS ON BUDGET OR LOGISTICS, WHERE WOULD YOU SEND THEM?

Friend:

Destination(s):

Where you'd have them stay:

Dishes and drinks you'd want them to try:

Sights you'd want them to see:

Activities you'd plan for them:

What else would you wish for them on their trip?

YELLOWSTONE
NATIONAL PARK,
UNITED STATES OF AMERICA

What do you find is the same everywhere you go?

PLACES TO SEE IN MY OWN COUNTRY

Sometimes you don't have to travel far to find adventure. Where do you most want to travel within your own country's borders, and why?

DOMESTIC
DEPARTURES

What would it be like to visit your home city as someone from another country?

_____

_____

_____

_____

_____

_____

_____

_____

_____

_____

_____

_____

_____

_____

_____

_____

_____

_____

_____

_____

_____

ARRIVALS
➡

JUST THE TICKET

How do you think travel will change in the next ten years? How about in twenty years, or more?

_____

_____

_____

_____

_____

_____

_____

_____

_____

_____

_____

_____

_____

_____

_____

_____

_____

_____

_____

_____

LEND A HAND

Try out the following ways to do good on the road and in the places you visit, and add in your own ideas at the end of the list.

- ☐ **ASSIST A FELLOW TRAVELER IN NEED OF HELP**

- ☐ **SWAP YOUR SEAT SO THAT TRAVELING COMPANIONS CAN SIT TOGETHER**

- ☐ **LEAVE A LARGE TIP (IN A PLACE WHERE TIPPING IS APPROPRIATE)**

- ☐ **BUY A COFFEE, DRINK, OR MEAL FOR SOMEONE YOU MEET ALONG THE WAY**

- ☐ **LEAVE A BOOK YOU'RE FINISHED WITH IN A FREE LIBRARY OR THE COMMON AREA OF WHERE YOU'RE STAYING**

- ☐ **SING THE PRAISES OF A RESTAURANT OR HOTEL EMPLOYEE TO THEIR BOSS**

- ☐ **DONATE MONEY OR TIME TO A CAUSE OR A NONPROFIT**

- ☐ _____

- ☐ _____

- ☐ _____

THE CODE OF THE TRAVELER

A TRAVELER MUST ALWAYS _____
_____

AND NEVER _____
_____

A TRAVELER SHOULD BE _____,
_____, AND _____

AND NOT _____, _____,
AND _____

BEFORE A TRIP, THE TRAVELER SHOULD _____
_____

WHILE TRAVELING, THEY MUST _____
_____

AND UPON ARRIVING HOME, THEY SHOULD _____
_____

IT'S IMPORTANT TO REMEMBER _____
_____

AND _____ IS ALWAYS IN GOOD TASTE

GLOBETROTTER CHALLENGE
LEVEL 3

- [ ] Get mistaken for a local while traveling

- [ ] Go on a solo trip

- [ ] Make a true friend from another place and keep in touch

- [ ] Fill a passport before it expires

- [ ] Complete an entire trip without speaking your native language except to your travel companions

- [ ] Fill in every page of this journal

TRAVEL SCRAPBOOK

FILL THESE PAGES WITH NOTES, PHOTOS, RECEIPTS, ADDRESSES FOR KEEPING IN TOUCH, AND ANY OTHER MEMORIES YOU'D LIKE TO PRESERVE FROM YOUR TRAVELS

ACKNOWLEDGMENTS

In February 2016, I got an out-of-the-blue email that changed my life— and I will be forever grateful to Marian Lizzi for sending it, for saying yes to my ideas, and for her expert editor's guidance that shaped this book into its better-than-I-ever-imagined final form. Huge thanks to Rachel Ayotte for all her help in getting the book to the finish line, to Lorie Pagnozzi and the design team for their help with the technical nitty-gritty, and to Dorian Hastings for her diligent copywriting. Thank you all so much for your help and guidance. It does take a village, and my village feels particularly solid!

I'm a lifelong travel addict, and an illustrator, and, as anyone reading this book will guess, a food-obsessed bottomless pit—but I have also had the exceedingly good fortune to be a student under some incredible teachers, and to combine travel with study in ways that shaped me into the person who would one day make this book. My sincerest thanks to Jackson Miller and Kathleen Spring of Linfield University, and to the teaching staff of AUCP Marseille, for opening the doors to international study and giving me the chance to start applying critical thinking to travel. Most of all, a massive and heartfelt ευχαριστώ to those who make the Fulbright Program possible; to Artemis Zenetou, Dimitrios Doutis, and the staff of Fulbright Greece; and to the staff and students of the American Farm School, whom I will forever think of as my giant Greek family. I learned so much from you all about what it means to truly get to know a place and culture, and my Greek year was one of the best of my life. Above all else, this book is an attempt to bring to others a little bit of what you gave to me.

I also owe many of my reference photos and page ideas to some particularly awesome trips with friends and family. To my mom, I will forever treasure my memories from our time in Paris! And to Josh, Ashley, Zelda, and Juniper Hale, thank you for being such excellent hosts and for introducing us to Hong Kong and China. May the unbelievable snacks and meals from that trip be forever remembered and honored in these pages.

And finally, to Nate, my public transit navigator, courageous stick-shift warrior of the Autobahn, and favorite travel buddy for life: if we can cross the street safely in Nha Trang, we can do anything. Here's to a lifetime of adventures—near and far, big and small—and to figuring it all out together. I will go literally anywhere if I get to go there with you!

ABOUT THE AUTHOR

Kate Peterson is a self-taught illustrator and the author of *You're Weird*. She lives and works in Boise, Idaho, with her husband and dog, and jumps at the chance to travel whenever she can.

For more of Kate's work, follow:

◎KATEPETERSONART

WWW.KATEPETERSON.ART

Also by
Kate Peterson

YOU'RE
WEIRD

A Creative Journal for **MISFITS**,
ODDBALLS, and Anyone Else
Who's Uniquely **AWESOME**

Kate Peterson

tarcherperigee